Using phonics

Mary Green

Acknowledgements

United Kingdom: Folens Publishers, Apex Business Centre, Boscombe Road, Dunstable, LU5 4RL.
Email: folens@folens.com

Ireland: Folens Publishers, Greenhills Road, Tallaght, Dublin 24.
Email: info@folens.ie

Poland: JUKA, ul. Renesansowa 38, Warsaw 01-905.

Editor: Jennifer Steele   Layout artist: Book Matrix, India   Illustrations: Lee Sullivan
Cover design: Holbrook Design   Cover image: Corbis

First published 2006 by Folens Limited.

British Library Cataloguing in Publication Data. A catalogue record for this publication is available from the British Library.

ISBN 1 84303 866 8 / 978 1 34303 866 5

Contents

Introduction   4

Adding endings   5
Endings (1)   6
Endings (2)   7
Endings (3)   8
Endings (4)   9
Asking questions   10

Blending consonants   11
Beginnings (1)   12
Beginnings (2)   13
Beginnings (3)   14
Beginnings (4)   15
Beginnings (5)   16

Vowels (1)   17
Saints and Stingrays   18
Find the words (1)   19
Find the words (2)   20
Adding 'e'   21
Look at the street   22

Vowels (2)   23
Peaches and cream   24
A crowd of words   25
Sound them out   26
Make a list   27
Tuesday blues   28

Vowels/compound words   29
Which sound?   30
Best foot forward   31
A starry night   32
Ready, steady, go!   33
A pair of words   34

Vowel sounds and 'r'   35
What can you remember?   36
Check your spelling   37
Sort them out   38
More sorting out   39
Get into gear   40

Triple blends/syllables   41
Making words   42
Danger!   43
Guessing game   44
Shaun Gaunt solves a problem   45
Lucky stars   46

Silent letters   47
Silent letters (1)   48
Silent letters (2)   49
Silent letters (3)   50
Silent letters (4)   51
Words with 'gue' or 'que'   52

Soft and hard sounds   53
The office   54
Grimini the Magician   55
Dolphins   56
That old chestnut   57
A toothache and a headache   58

Prefixes and suffixes   59
Prefix meanings   60
Prefixes   61
Suffixes   62
Syllable linking   63

Assessment sheet   64

Introduction

Specials! *English Using phonics* provides a series of Activity sheets for those students who have entered secondary school but still find reading challenging. They will almost certainly have acquired some reading skills but may find it difficult to make further progress without being taught a range of sound patterns.

Each unit focuses on a particular sound or skill and these increase in difficulty, for example: 'Adding endings', 'Blending consonants', 'Vowels' and so on. However, the book is not a course in itself. It is meant to support the reading approach that the teacher already uses. This may involve 'synthetic phonics', for example. It may be a fast-track approach or a more detailed programme, depending on the student's needs. The teacher can select those Activity sheets from which the student will benefit, and, where applicable, particular sounds within Activity sheets.

It should also be emphasised that phonics should not be used in isolation. It is an aspect of reading, not the skill in itself. Students should have access to good literature, fiction and non-fiction and other reading materials, which they can read alone or have read to them.

The Teacher's notes give guidance and are laid out as follows:

Learning objectives

These are the main skills or knowledge to be learned.

Prior knowledge

This refers to the minimum skills or knowledge required by students to complete the tasks. As a rule, students should have a reading comprehension age of six to nine years and should be working at levels 1 to 3. Some student pages are more challenging than others and will need to be selected accordingly.

English Framework links

All units link to aspects of the English Framework at Key Stage 3 and details are given.

Scottish attainment targets

Links are given to the Scottish 5–14 National Guidelines.

Background

This gives additional information for the teacher about particular sound patterns.

Starter activity

Since the units can be taught as a lesson, a warm-up activity focusing on an aspect of the unit is suggested.

Activity sheets

Suggestions for using the Activity sheets are given here. Different approaches are sometimes given or links with other Activity sheets.

Plenary

The teacher can use the suggestions here to do additional work, recap on the main points covered or reinforce a particular sound.

Assessment sheet

At the end of the book is an Assessment sheet focusing on student progress. It can be used in different ways. A student could complete it as self-assessment, while his or her teacher also completes one on the student's progress. The two can then be compared. This is useful in situations where the teacher or classroom assistant is working with one student. Alternatively, students could work in partners to carry out peer assessments and then compare the outcomes with each other.

Starting from a simple base that students can manage, the Assessment sheet allows the student to discuss his or her own progress, consider different points of view, discuss how he or she might improve and allow the teacher to see the work from the student's perspective. A completed sample assessment sheet is given here.

Assessment sheet

Tick the boxes to show what you know or what you can do

	Know/ Yes	Not sure/ Sometimes	Don't know/ No
1. I listen to the teacher.	✓		
2. I can work well with a partner.		✓	
3. I can work well in a group.			✓
4. I know the word endings -dd,-ff,-ll.	✓		
5. I know the word endings -lk, -ld, -ng.		✓	
6. I can write sentences using full stops and capital letters.	✓		
7. I can use 'wh' sounds to write questions.			✓

I know best / I can do best: ....
....

I need to: (Write no more than three targets.)
....
....
....

Teacher's notes

Adding endings

Objectives

- Learn the double consonant word endings: 'ck', 'dd', 'ff', 'gg', 'll', 'ss'
- Learn and blend the final consonant blends: 'th', 'ch', 'lk', 'ld', 'ng', 'nd'; 'sk', 'lp', 'mp', 'sp', 'ct', 'ft'; 'lt', 'nt', 'st', 'nk', 'xt', 'pt', 'lf'
- Write simple sentences using full stops and capital letters
- Use 'wh' sounds to read, answer and write questions using question marks

Prior knowledge

Students should be able to blend simple CVC (consonant/vowel/consonant) words such as 'cat' and read them separately in context and spell them. They should know the alphabet and its short sounds and should be able to write simple sentences.

English Framework links

Yr7 Word level 1; Yr8 Word level 1; Yr9 Word level 1

Scottish attainment targets

English Language – Writing
Strand – Spelling
Level C
Strand – Punctuation and structure
Level C

Background

Once students can read CVC words, they can tackle double consonant endings and final consonant blends. If they have good reading experience there may be several endings that they know already and you can use the relevant Activity sheets for consolidation. You can also use the Activity sheets to note those sounds they are less sure of and focus on them. (You may wish to teach initial consonant blends before tackling endings. If so, please see the unit, 'Blending consonants'.)

Starter activity

Explain to or remind students that when we read we blend sounds together to make words and that this can help us to tackle words of which we are unsure. Go through CVC examples and also some double consonant word endings, such as 'call', 'fall' and 'hall', before beginning the first Activity sheet.

Activity sheets

It is unlikely that you will use all the Activity sheets in one session and it will not be necessary for them to be completed by students who can do them easily. The words on the first Activity sheet, 'Endings (1)', only require students to blend three sounds as they would with a CVC word. However, the Activity sheet can also be used for spelling practice. Ensure that the students say all the words and complete the written examples before any spelling test.

In the Activity sheets, 'Endings (2)', '(3)' and '(4)', help students to blend the sound with the whole word. They should do this regularly as they read or write the words. Students should try to complete the sentences on their own initially on the last of these sheets.

The final Activity sheet, 'Asking questions', can be used for discussion and expanded to cover other issues, according to the students' abilities. Emphasise the importance of 'wh' words as question words and the use of the question mark. Students should work in groups, but should try to write their own questions.

Plenary

Ask students in one group to read out their questions; students in another group can answer them. Carry out spot checks on words and sounds, particularly those that cause problems. You can make quick, simple matching tasks to accommodate some of these words, using the same vowel sound, for example:

Activity sheet – Adding endings

Endings (1)

☞ Match the picture to the word, then to the word again.
The first one has been done for you.

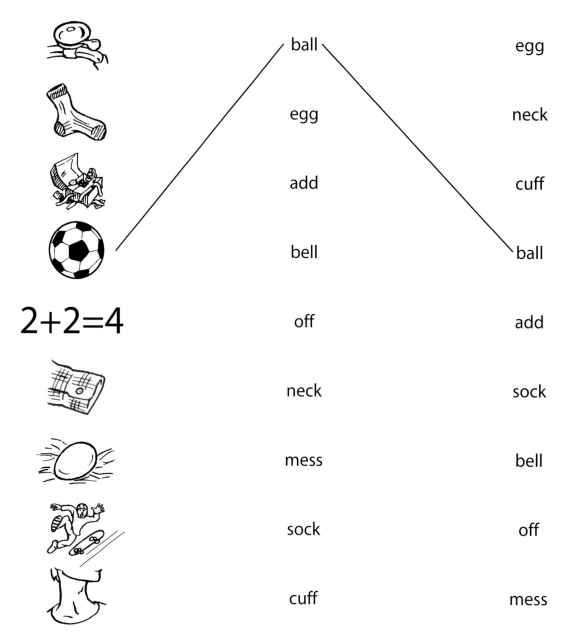

ball		egg
egg		neck
add		cuff
bell		ball
off		add
neck		sock
mess		bell
sock		off
cuff		mess

☞ Choose from the words above to finish the words in the file card.

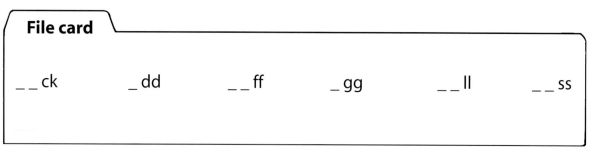

File card

_ _ ck   _ dd   _ _ ff   _ gg   _ _ ll   _ _ ss

English Using phonics

Endings (2)

☞ Write these words in the correct file cards.

- ring   path   gold   milk   pond   with
- silk   rich   sing   which   hold   hand

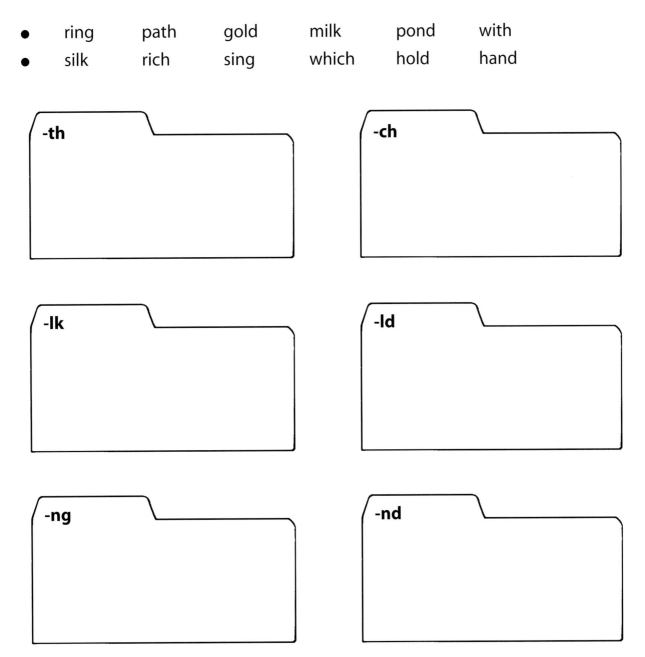

-th

-ch

-lk

-ld

-ng

-nd

☞ Read these words. Add them to the file cards.

- song   held   Goth   sand   sulk   much

☞ Think of more words with the same endings. Add them to the file cards.

English Using phonics

Endings (3)

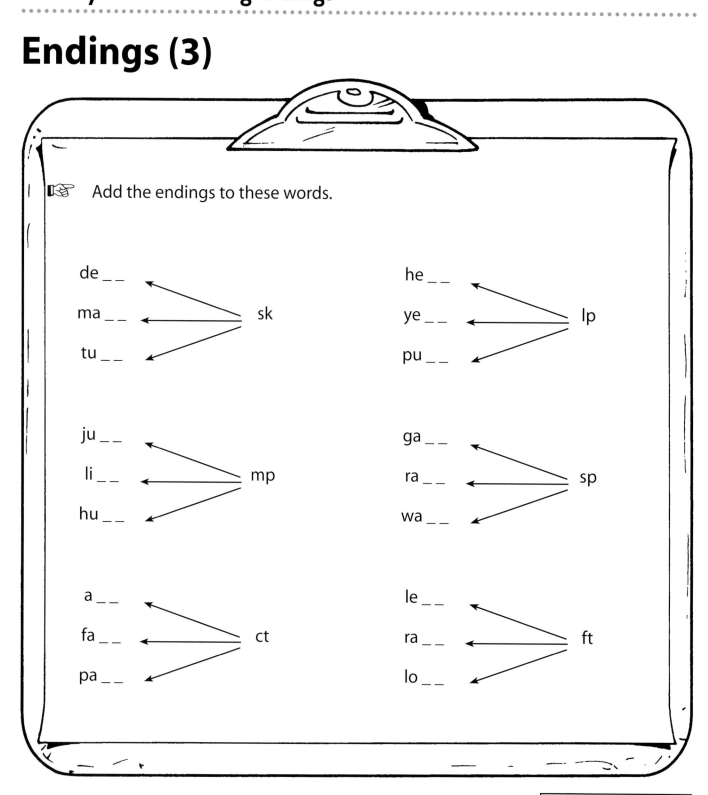

☞ Add the endings to these words.

de _ _
ma _ _   sk
tu _ _

he _ _
ye _ _   lp
pu _ _

ju _ _
li _ _   mp
hu _ _

ga _ _
ra _ _   sp
wa _ _

a _ _
fa _ _   ct
pa _ _

le _ _
ra _ _   ft
lo _ _

☞ Finish these sentences.

Choose from the words you made above.

1. He will _ _ _ in the play.
2. The dog gave a _ _ _ _ .
3. He has hurt his _ _ _ _ foot.

    English Using phonics

Endings (4)

☞ Add the endings to these words.

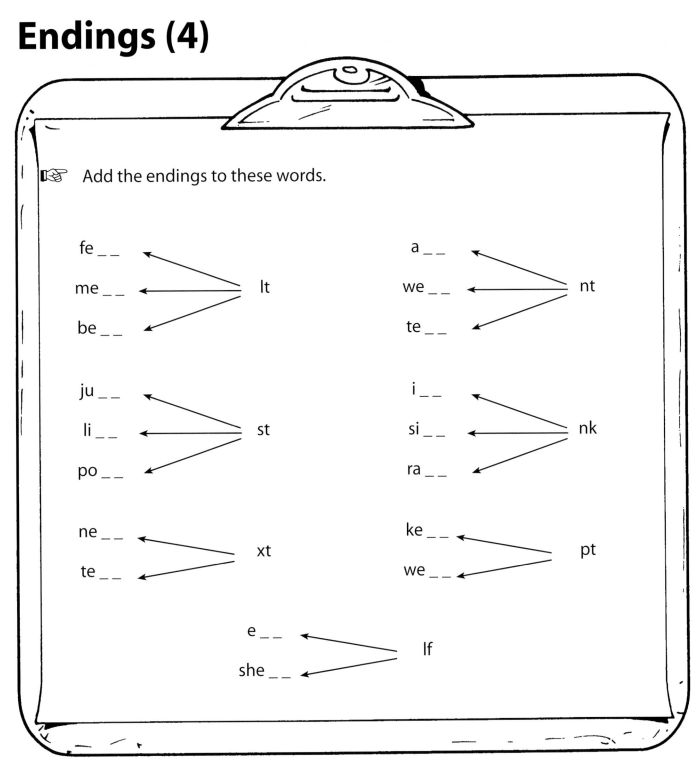

fe _ _
me _ _   lt
be _ _

a _ _
we _ _   nt
te _ _

ju _ _
li _ _   st
po _ _

i _ _
si _ _   nk
ra _ _

ne _ _   xt
te _ _

ke _ _   pt
we _ _

e _ _   lf
she _ _

☞ Write four sentences using some of the words above and words of your own.

1. The _____
2. A _____
3. She _____
4. He _____

Asking questions

☞ Read and answer the questions about the picture.

1. Who is shouting?

_____

2. Why do you think they are shouting?

_____

3. What time is it?

_____

4. Where is the girl?

_____

5. Which boy is playing darts?

_____

6. When do you think the club closes?

_____

☞ Now write five questions of your own.

Use Who? Why? What? Where? Which? or When?

1. _____

2. _____

3. _____

4. _____

5. _____

● Ask your partner to answer them.

Teacher's notes

Blending consonants

Objectives

- Learn and blend the initial consonant blends: 'bl','cl','fl';'pl','sl','gl';'br','cr','dr';'sm','sn','sp','st','sw', 'tw','dw';'fr','gr','pr','tr','sc','sk'
- Write simple sentences using full stops and capital letters
- Read short texts and identify words containing blends the students have learned

Prior knowledge

Students should be able to blend simple CVC (consonant/vowel/consonant) sounds, including most double consonant endings, read them separately and in context and should be able to write in sentences.

English Framework links

Yr7 Word level 1; Yr8 Word level 1; Yr9 Word level 1

Scottish attainment targets

English Language – Writing
Strand – Spelling
Level C
English Language – Reading
Strand – Reading aloud
Level B

Background

Students may already have grasped that two sounds can be combined to produce one, even if they are uncertain of them. Here, however, they can still hear both consonant sounds and it is useful to remind them of this and to listen for them as they blend the sounds.

Starter activity

Introduce the **keyword** 'blend' and remind students that when we read, we blend sounds together to make words. Explain that this can help us to tackle words of which we are unsure. Go through CVC examples and also some double consonant word endings (for example, 'ca*ll*', 'fa*ll*' and 'ha*ll*') with students before beginning the first Activity sheet.

Activity sheets

All the common initial blends are given in the Activity sheets, 'Beginnings (1)' to '(5)'. Work through the sheets or select to suit your purpose, encouraging students to read the words several times over. Discuss the meanings of any words students do not know after they have finished each sheet. They may be unfamiliar with: 'glum', 'grim' and 'prank'. These can be recorded in students' word banks. You can also ask students to think of further words, focusing on particular blends.

At the end of the final Activity sheet, 'Beginnings (5)', students are asked to read a short passage. This includes all of the consonant blends on that page and one or two others. It also includes consonant endings, most of which are covered in the previous unit, 'Adding endings'. Students can revisit any blends and endings of which they are uncertain.

Plenary

Recap on the blends covered. You can make jigsaw blends, consisting of a series of cards with blends to be matched with other parts of words, also written on cards. For example:

Give students a time limit to make as many words as they can.

Activity sheet – Blending consonants

Beginnings (1)

☞ Write these words. Say them as you write.

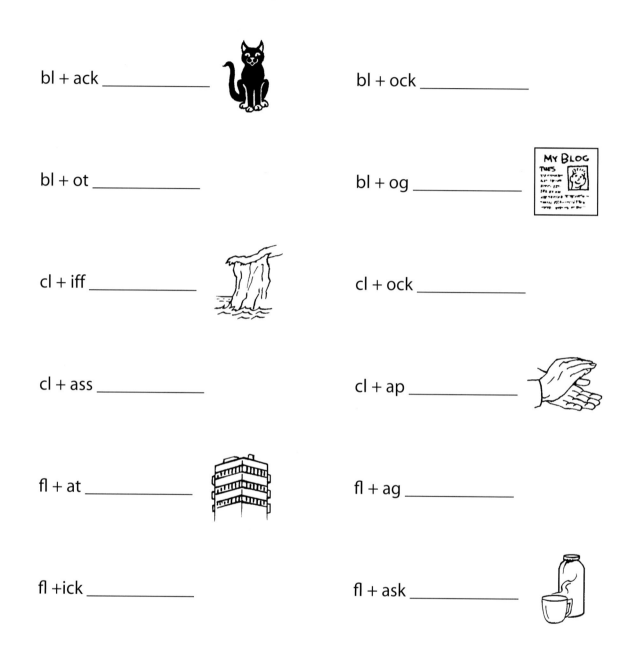

bl + ack _____

bl + ock _____

bl + ot _____

bl + og _____

cl + iff _____

cl + ock _____

cl + ass _____

cl + ap _____

fl + at _____

fl + ag _____

fl +ick _____

fl + ask _____

☞ Write the words under the correct heading and read them.

bl	cl	fl
_____	_____	_____
_____	_____	_____
_____	_____	_____
_____	_____	_____

English Using phonics

© Folens (copiable page)

Activity sheet – Blending consonants

Beginnings (2)

☞ Match the picture to the word, then to the word again. Next, write the blend in the column. The first one has been done for you.

Blends

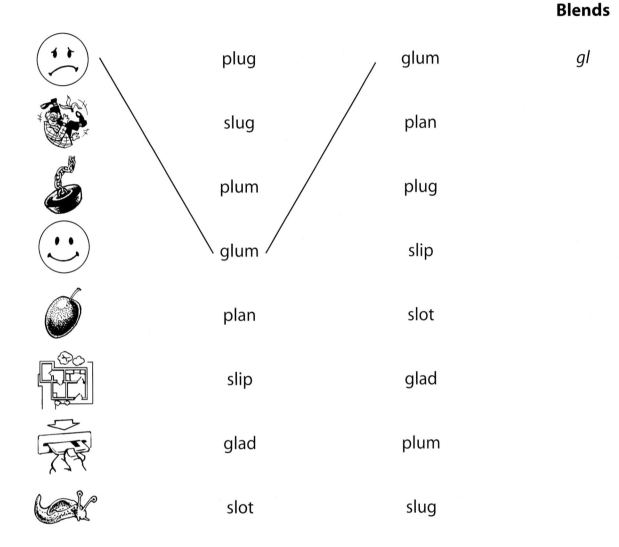

plug	glum	*gl*
slug	plan	
plum	plug	
glum	slip	
plan	slot	
slip	glad	
glad	plum	
slot	slug	

☞ Write these words under the correct heading and read them.

● plank   slosh   gloss   glint   sling   plant   glass   plump   slant

pl   **sl**   **gl**

_____   _____   _____

_____   _____   _____

_____   _____   _____

Activity sheet – Blending consonants

Beginnings (3)

☞ Write down the correct blends to make words. Use the pictures to help you.
Read the words.

- Blends: **br**   **cr**   **dr**

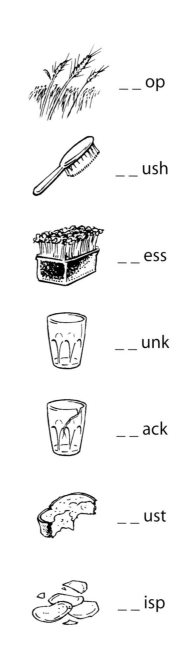

_ _ op

_ _ op

_ _ ush

_ _ ush

_ _ ess

_ _ ess

_ _ amp

_ _ unk

_ _ im

_ _ ack

_ _ and

_ _ ust

_ _ ip

_ _ isp

☞ Finish the sentences, using these words.

- drag   drums   crab

1. Put the _____ back in the pool.

2. Can he _____ the case up the hill?

3. He plays the _____ in the band.

English Using phonics   © Folens (copiable page)

Beginnings (4)

☞ Add beginnings to these words. Read the words.

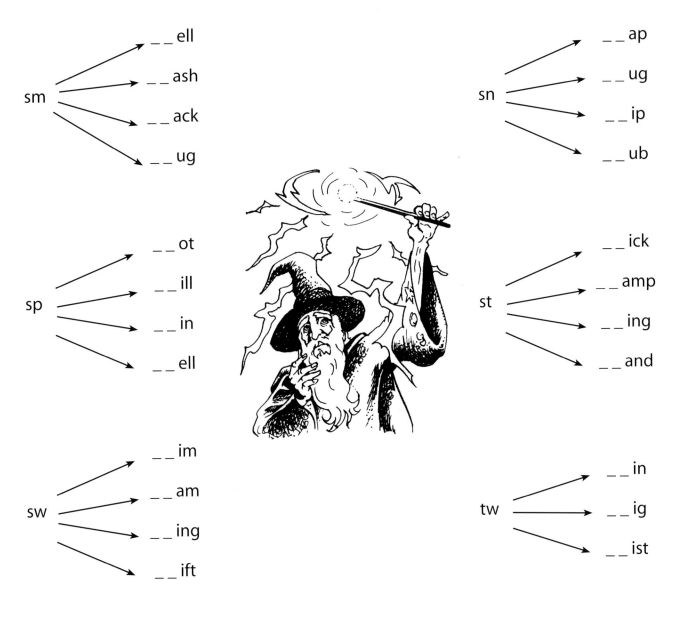

sm
- _ _ ell
- _ _ ash
- _ _ ack
- _ _ ug

sn
- _ _ ap
- _ _ ug
- _ _ ip
- _ _ ub

sp
- _ _ ot
- _ _ ill
- _ _ in
- _ _ ell

st
- _ _ ick
- _ _ amp
- _ _ ing
- _ _ and

sw
- _ _ im
- _ _ am
- _ _ ing
- _ _ ift

tw
- _ _ in
- _ _ ig
- _ _ ist

dw + ell _ _ _ _ _

☞ Write three sentences, using words on this page.

1._____

2._____

3._____

Beginnings (5)

☞ Write these words. Say them as you write.

fr + esh _____

fr + og _____

gr + in _____

gr + im _____

pr + int _____

pr + ank _____

tr + im _____

tr + uck _____

sc + arf _____

sc + am _____

sk + ip _____

sk + im _____

sk + id _____

sk + ill _____

☞ Read the following. Underline any words you do not know. Discuss these words with a partner.

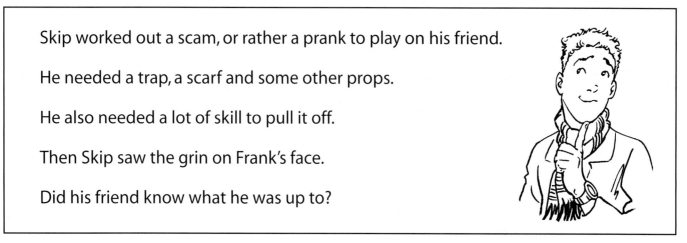

Skip worked out a scam, or rather a prank to play on his friend.

He needed a trap, a scarf and some other props.

He also needed a lot of skill to pull it off.

Then Skip saw the grin on Frank's face.

Did his friend know what he was up to?

Teacher's notes

Vowels (1)

Objectives

- Learn the long vowel phonemes 'ai', 'ay'; 'oa', 'ow', 'oe'; 'ie', 'y', 'igh'; 'a-e', 'e-e', 'i-e', 'o-e', 'u-e'; 'ee', 'oo'
- Write simple sentences using full stops and capital letters

Prior knowledge

Students should be able to blend some initial consonant blends and endings and be able to write sentences. They should be able to spell three- and four-letter words.

English Framework links

Yr7 Word level 1; Yr8 Word level 1; Yr9 Word level 1

Scottish attainment targets

English Language – Writing
Strand – Spelling
Level C
Strand – Punctuation and structure
Level C

Background

This unit covers most of the long vowel phonemes students need to know to make progress. They need to grasp that two sounds:

- can be combined to make one
- that the same sound can be produced in different combinations (for example, 'ai' and 'ay' produce the same long vowel sound)
- that this is a common feature of many words.

Starter activity

Check that all students can discriminate sounds. Read aloud a series of words containing the same sound except for one example, such as 'train/bay/tray/room/pain/lane'. Make this into a rhyming game. Ask students to listen for the rhyming words and choose the odd one out. Note if any students have difficulty and check them again later. They may have difficulty with particular sounds only, but if you are alerted to any difficulties, you will need to investigate further. Emphasising a multi-sensory approach may help.

Ask those students who have been successful to think of other words with similar sounds (for example, 'ai' and long 'oo').

Activity sheets

Before beginning the first three Activity sheets:

- rehearse each phoneme
- emphasise the difference between the sound and the spelling of the words, if you wish to use focus on spelling.

The first three Activity sheets, 'Saints and Stingrays' and 'Find the words (1)' and '(2)', can be done in any order and you can select which need to be done. Once students have completed each sheet, note who has difficulty and where. In 'Find the words (1)' and '(2)', the chosen words have digraphs that come from earlier units and should be within the students' experience.

The Activity sheet, 'Adding 'e'', explains the change in the central vowel from short to long. Remind students that the added 'e' is silent. Some students may find this rhyme useful:

Remember this rhyme, 123,
The vowel sounds its name
When you add an 'e'.

On the final Activity sheet, 'Look at the street', students need to identify and list words containing 'ee' and 'oo'.

Plenary

Recap on the sounds covered, then read the following limerick to students, asking them to identify the 'oo' and 'ui' words:

There once was a tailor called Poots,
Who only made tight-fitting suits.
So as soon as you laughed,
The seams fell apart,
And all that was left were your boots.

Activity sheet – Vowels (1)

Saints and Stingrays

☞ Say these words and write them under the correct teams.

way	sail	day	play	chain	paid	clay	again	brain	nail	today	plain
stay	may	gain	tray	pain	jay	mail	sway	slay	vain	away	drain

The Saints
ai

The Stingrays
ay

English Using phonics

Find the words (1)

☞ Read these words and put a ring round the 'oa' words.

☞ Read these words and put a ring round the 'ow' words.

oa

ball	neck	rain	goat	mask
egg	fast	toast	next	coat
boat	what	grin	coach	day
snap	sail	toad	when	slip

ow

brush	snow	skim	truck	grow
drink	twig	crow	blow	plug
below	fresh	snug	lamp	flow
snack	fact	gasp	green	limp

☞ Read these words and put a ring round the 'oe' words.

oe

twins	snake	cross	tree	Joe
last	long	toe	sing	hand
pink	crush	doe	glass	plant
glint	foe	swing	play	gain

☞ Now write the words you have ringed under the correct heading.
Say each word. Remember they all have the same sound.

oa	ow	oe
_____	_____	_____
_____	_____	_____
_____	_____	_____
_____	_____	_____
_____	_____	_____

Find the words (2)

☞ Read these words and put a ring round the 'ie' words.

☞ Read these words and put a ring round the 'igh' words.

ie				
trunk	crab	pie	from	drop
step	lie	stick	left	damp
cuff	die	sock	full	yell
ant	list	tie	help	elf

igh				
flag	glad	high	clip	crash
sigh	spade	spot	swim	light
link	pond	fight	silk	went
night	lend	shelf	task	ring

☞ Read these words and put a ring round the 'y' words.

y				
plum	cry	clock	Spain	text
sulk	sack	dry	land	ask
mend	luck	fresh	why	fly
trap	spy	crisp	shy	fling

☞ Now write the words you have ringed under the correct heading.
   Say each word. Remember they all have the same sound.

ie	igh	y
_____	_____	_____
_____	_____	_____
_____	_____	_____
_____	_____	_____
		_____

English Using phonics

Adding 'e'

☞ Look at the following.

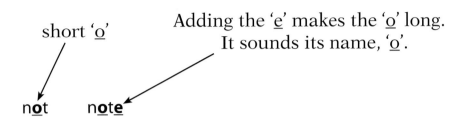

short 'o'

Adding the 'e' makes the 'o' long.
It sounds its name, 'o'.

n**o**t   n**ote**

- All the vowels, a e i o u, change their sounds like this.
  Change these words by adding 'e'. Write them again in full.
  Read them with a partner.

cod _____   rip _____   mat _____

pin _____   pan _____   hat _____

cut _____   hop _____   pip _____

bit _____   tub _____   dot _____

cub _____   rat _____   rod _____

pop _____   win _____   pet _____

☞ Write four sentences using some of the words. Try to use more than one word in a sentence, like this: **Pete** and his **mate** worked out the **code**.

1. _____

   _____

2. _____

   _____

3. _____

   _____

4. _____

   _____

Look at the street

☞ Write the headings 'ee' and 'oo' on another sheet of paper.

Look at the illustration and find words with 'ee' and 'oo'.

Write the words under the correct heading.

English Using phonics

Teacher's notes

Vowels (2)

Objectives

- Learn the vowel phonemes 'ea' (as in 'sea'); 'ow' (as in 'cow'); 'ou' (as in 'cloud'); 'oi','oy'; 'ew','ue','ui'
- Deduce meanings
- Read a short text
- Write simple sentences using full stops and capital letters

Prior knowledge

Students should be able to blend initial consonant blends, endings and know some long vowel phonemes. They should be able to write sentences and spell some of the words they have learned.

English Framework links

Yr7 Word level 1; Yr8 Word level 1; Yr9 Word level 1

Scottish attainment targets

English Language – Writing
Strand – Spelling
Level C
English Language – Reading
Strand – Reading to reflect on the writer's ideas and craft
Level B

Background

Once students know some vowel phonemes, they can pick up others. In this unit there are further vowel phonemes, some of which students may have learned incidentally. Continue to emphasise that two sounds can be combined to make one and that the same sound can be produced in different combinations.

Starter activity

Check students' spelling by giving them a range of phonemes that they've covered, even if the focus has been reading. You may also like to check their handwriting, noting whether they have good pen control and the speed with which they write, since this aids spelling.

Activity sheets

Rehearse with students the phonemes you wish to focus on before they begin the Activity sheets.

Students could work in pairs to complete the first three Activity sheets, 'Peaches and cream', 'A crowd of words' and 'Sound them out'. Students should know the meanings of most words but will need to deduce which clues fit each word, rather like the clues of a crossword. Note who can work them out and who has difficulty. The sheets can be done in any order. Ensure students can repeat the phonemes before they begin. You may need to read the clues to students.

In the Activity sheet, 'Make a list', students are dealing with different letter combinations that produce the same sound. They should work on their own to do this as far as possible.

In the final Activity sheet, 'Tuesday blues', students should work in pairs again. This is a more challenging sheet and students must make sense of the whole text. They will need to use the context, their grammar knowledge and word recognition, as well as sound, to make good guesses. They can take it in turns to read the completed text to each other, noting any words they do not know.

Plenary

Recap the sounds covered. The game 'Snap' can be played using matching word cards or by grouping words according to their sound. The cards can then be wiped and used again.

Peaches and cream

☞ Add 'ea' to these words and say them.
Then match the words to the clues.
The first one has been done for you.

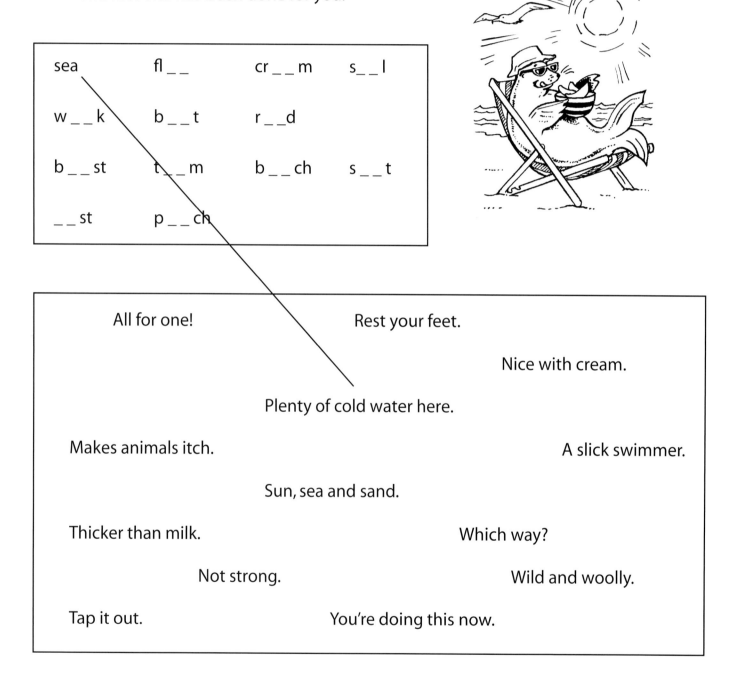

sea	fl _ _	cr _ _ m	s _ _ l
w _ _ k	b _ _ t	r _ _ d	
b _ _ st	t _ _ m	b _ _ ch	s _ _ t
_ _ st	p _ _ ch		

All for one!   Rest your feet.

                                 Nice with cream.

                  Plenty of cold water here.

Makes animals itch.   A slick swimmer.

                  Sun, sea and sand.

Thicker than milk.   Which way?

            Not strong.   Wild and woolly.

Tap it out.   You're doing this now.

☞ Now think of four more words with the 'ea' sound.

_____   _____

_____   _____

Activity sheet – Vowels (2)

A crowd of words

☞ Add 'ow' to these words and say them.
Then match the words to the clues
The first one has been done for you.

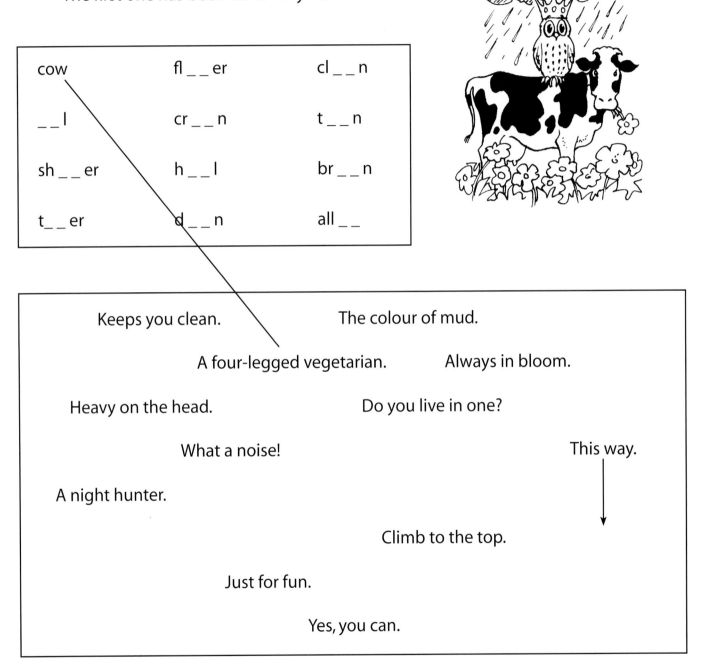

cow	fl _ _ er	cl _ _ n
_ _ l	cr _ _ n	t _ _ n
sh _ _ er	h _ _ l	br _ _ n
t _ _ er	d _ _ n	all _ _

Keeps you clean.   The colour of mud.

A four-legged vegetarian.   Always in bloom.

Heavy on the head.   Do you live in one?

What a noise!   This way.

A night hunter.

Climb to the top.

Just for fun.

Yes, you can.

☞ Think of three more words with the 'ow' sound.

_____   _____

_____

English Using phonics

Sound them out

☞ Add 'ou' to these words and say them.
Then match the words to the clues.
The first one has been done for you.

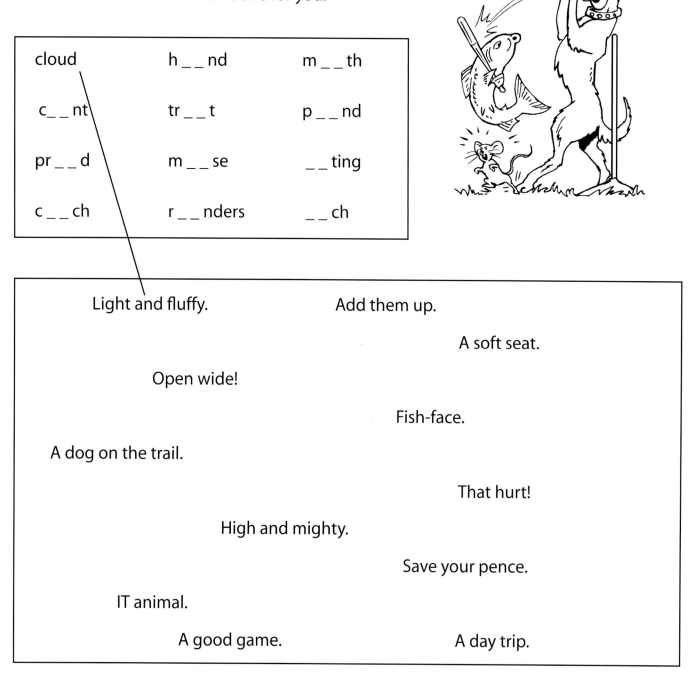

cloud	h _ _ nd	m _ _ th
c _ _ nt	tr _ _ t	p _ _ nd
pr _ _ d	m _ _ se	_ _ ting
c _ _ ch	r _ _ nders	_ _ ch

Light and fluffy.

Add them up.

A soft seat.

Open wide!

Fish-face.

A dog on the trail.

That hurt!

High and mighty.

Save your pence.

IT animal.

A good game.

A day trip.

☞ Think of three more words with the 'ou' sound.

_____   _____

_____

English Using phonics

Make a list

☞ Say these words and write them under the correct lists.

boy	foil	soil	toy	coin	oil	joy
coil	loyal	royal	point	join	enjoy	
Troy	boil	noise	soya	spoil	voice	
joyful	choice	Roy	joint	moist		

oi

oy

☞ Write sentences with both words in them.

1. **oil**   **spoiled**   The car _____

_____

2. **boil**   **foil**   Put _____

_____

3. **voice** **noise**   Jack _____

_____

Activity sheet – Vowels (2)

Tuesday blues

☞ Read the web diary below. The missing words are in the word bank. Working with a partner, write in the missing words in the web diary.

Diary entry for _____

What an awful day! Here's why.

Homework was _____ today. I forgot it. Anyway I didn't have

a _____ how to do it. Miss A _____ made me put my

_____ gum in the bin. Lunch was _____ and _____ .

All I wanted was chips. I spilled glue on Mr S _____ shoes.

Then I tripped. It went all over his _____ . Mark said I _____

his work on the floor. Not _____ ! Mark _____ up my

work. Kept in till 5pm. Just got home. The dog has _____

my _____ trainers!

Word bank

due	new	Andrews	fruit	clue	true	chewing
stew	screwed	suit	threw	Tuesday	chewed	Stewart's

☞ Take it in turns to read the completed text with your partner, noting any words you do not know.

Teacher's notes

Vowels/compound words

Objectives

- Learn the vowel phonemes 'y' as the long vowel sound 'e'; 'u' (short), 'oo' (short); the vowel consonant 'ar'; the short vowel sound 'ea'
- Create compound words
- Write a short paragraph

Prior knowledge

Students should know a range of blends and phonemes. They should be able to read short texts confidently, write sentences and spell some of the words they have learned to read.

English Framework links

Yr7 Word level 1; Yr8 Word level 1; Yr9 Word level 1

Scottish attainment targets

English Language – Writing
Strand – Punctuation and structure
Level C
Strand – Knowledge about language
Level D

Background

This unit contains a range of different sounds, including short and long vowel sounds and the vowel consonant 'ar', in which the 'r' affects the vowel sound (see also the unit, 'Vowel sounds and 'r''). If students are making good progress they may find they can read words with sounds they have not been formally taught. Indeed, they can often read more than they think. They can also cope with learning more sounds over a short period of time. However, their spelling performance will often lag behind. For example, in words that include 'ar' (and 'er', 'or', 'ir' and 'ur') the 'r' is sometimes omitted. It is therefore useful to include some regular spelling work on the words that students are learning.

Starter activity

Refer back to the unit, 'Vowels (1)' and ask students what sounds 'y' has. If necessary, remind them that it has a long 'i' vowel ending, as well as a consonant sound (see the Activity sheet, 'Find the words (2)'). Ask students to recall examples. Explain that it also has another long vowel sound, 'e', and lead into the first Activity sheet, 'Which sound?'.

Activity sheets

Students are asked to identify the correct 'y' sound by identifying the rhyming words. Encourage them to do this in other similar situations. If students are coping well, you may wish to introduce the medial 'y' sound (as in 'nylon' and 'python'). 'Y' also has a short 'y' sound (for example, 'syrup').

The Activity sheets, 'Best foot forward' and 'A starry night', deal with the short vowel sounds 'u' (pull) and 'oo' (good), and the 'ar' sound. In the Activity sheet, 'A starry night', read the clues to students. The short 'ea' sound (for example, head) is often harder for students to recall, especially in two or more syllable words. However, encourage them to read the sentences in the Activity sheet, 'Ready, steady, go!', on their own as far as possible and identify the sounds.

In 'A pair of words', students are asked to identify compound words and also to create their own. They could decide on interesting definitions with partners. Point out to students that many new words enter the language by combining two words to make one and in this way language is constantly growing and changing. When the worksheet is complete, you may wish to remind students to distinguish between the long 'oo' (boot) and the short 'oo'. (When copying the page enlarge it to A3 size.)

Plenary

Recap on the sounds covered, focusing on any that have proved tricky. Students can carry out peer assessments and assemble future targets.

Activity sheet – Vowels/compound words

Which sound?

Remember 'y' can sound like 'i': fl**y**.

It has other sounds too. It can sound like 'e': bab**y**.

☞ Draw arrows to link the words that rhyme with 'baby'.
Cross out the words that don't rhyme with 'baby'.

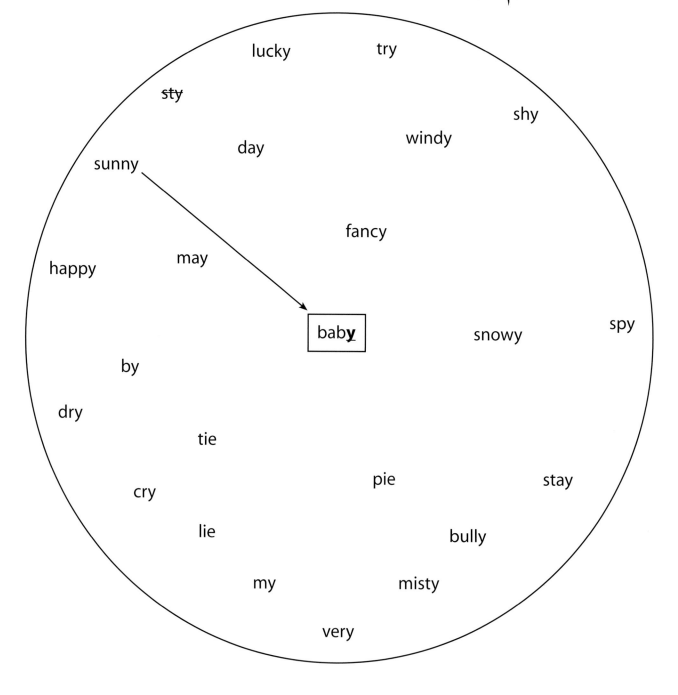

lucky

try

~~sty~~

shy

windy

day

sunny

fancy

happy   may

bab**y**   snowy   spy

by

dry

tie

pie   stay

cry

lie   bully

my   misty

very

English Using phonics   © Folens (copiable page)

Best foot forward

☞ Say these words and write them under the correct lists.

good	wood	soot	put	stood
pull	hood	book	look	full
took	brook	foot	hook	putting
bull	rook	shook	fuller	nook

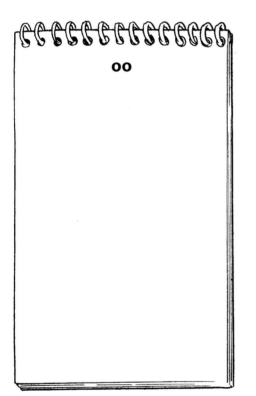

oo

u

☞ Write a paragraph. Include these words:

brook   hook   foot   putting

One day _____

Suddenly _____

Then _____

Finally _____

English Using phonics

Activity sheet – Vowels/compound words

A starry night

☞ Add 'ar' to these words and say them.
Then match the words to the clues.
The first one has been done for you.

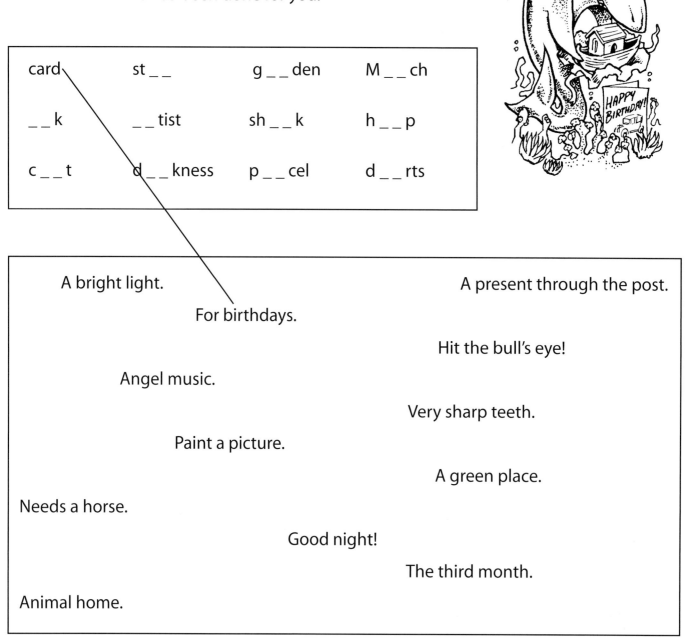

card	st _ _	g _ _ den	M _ _ ch
_ _ k	_ _ tist	sh _ _ k	h _ _ p
c _ _ t	d _ _ kness	p _ _ cel	d _ _ rts

A bright light.

For birthdays.

A present through the post.

Hit the bull's eye!

Angel music.

Very sharp teeth.

Paint a picture.

A green place.

Needs a horse.

Good night!

The third month.

Animal home.

☞ Think of three more words with the 'ar' sound.

_____   _____

_____

English Using phonics

Activity sheet – Vowels/compound words

Ready, steady, go!

Remember 'ea' can sound its name: 'e', as in 't**ea**'.
It is a long 'e'.

It has other sounds too.
It can have a short 'e' sound, as in 'h**ea**d'.

What are the 'ea' sounds in this sentence?

- **Ea**t your br**ea**d and butter.

☞ Underline only the words that have the <u>short</u> 'ea' sound.

1.   We have to go now! Are you ready?

2.   The sweater was full of tiny moth holes.

3.   Spread the picnic food out. We'll have a feast.

4.   Please leave the parrot alone! It's cleaning its feathers.

5.   The teacher put all the books into the box, but it was too heavy to lift.

6.   The spy held up the tube of deadly poison. It was a useful weapon.

7.   Instead of going to Blackpool they went to Spain, where it rained.

☞ Think of four more words with the <u>short</u> 'ea' sound.

_____   _____

_____   _____

- Write a sentence containing some of your words.

_____

A pair of words

We can put two words together to make one.
This becomes a compound word:

- class + room = classroom.

☞ Make compound words from these.
Write them underneath.

bow   noon   pet   pop   to   corn   key   car   day   hole   after   rain

☞ Cut out the cards below. Pair them up to make up your own compound words.
Tell a partner what they mean. For example, 'rainjar' for catching water.

rain	nip	spell	glass	boot
ear	jar	sun	rail	charm
key	hot	bag	wind	book
side	tail	bike	leap	toe

English Using phonics   © Folens (copiable page)

Teacher's notes

Vowel sounds and 'r'

Objectives

● Learn the vowel phonemes: 'er'/'ir'/'ur'
● Learn the short vowel phonemes: 'air'/'are'/'ear'
● Learn the vowel phonemes: 'or'/'oor'/'ore'/'oar'
● Learn the long vowel phoneme: 'ear'

Prior knowledge

Students should be able to synthesise a range of phoneme blends and endings. They should be able to write sentences and spell some of the words they have learned.

English Framework links

Yr7 Word level 1; Yr8 Word level 1; Yr9 Word level 1

Scottish attainment targets

English Language – Writing
Strand – Spelling
Level C

Background

The Activity sheets in this unit focus on a series of vowel sounds affected by the consonant 'r'. They can be learned as letter strings, as well as sounds, particularly if students are being taught to spell the words. Many students, for example, spell 'ir' and 'ur' words using 'er'. There are others that are not explored here, for example 'ire' in words such as 'fire', 'ear' in words such as 'heart' and 'ure' in words such as 'sure'. You may wish to tackle words with these sounds too. See also the Activity sheet, 'A starry night', in the unit, 'Vowels/compound words'.

Starter activity

Note whether students can read some of the 'or' words in their various letter patterns. If they recognise most of them you can use the unit to focus on spelling and spelling families only.

Activity sheets

Introduce the 'er'/'ir'/'ur' sound and ask students to learn and classify the words in the Activity sheet, 'What can you remember?'. You can then split the Activity sheet in two and ask students to complete the sentences without referring to the words. Do the same with the next Activity sheet, 'Check your spelling'. Work on homophones is also included.

The Activity sheets 'Sort them out' and 'More sorting out' both deal with the numerous letter combinations for the 'or' sound. The focus here is on spelling (although the words can be used to reinforce reading) and tips are given for remembering words. It is best to give these sheets separately, rather than tackle all the combinations at once.

The last Activity sheet deals with 'ear' as the long vowel sound 'eer' (as in 'near') and has been separated from the short vowel sound 'ear' (as in 'bear'). Students often confuse words that have the same spelling but a different sound (homonyms). An example in this unit, which you may wish to refer to, is the word 'tear'.

Plenary

If students have performed well you may like to give them a series of new words from the same word families as those they have covered. You could ask them either to read them as separate words, unaided by context, or to spell them.

Activity sheet – Vowel sounds and 'r'

What can you remember?

Remember, although these words all have an 'er' sound, they are not spelled the same: t**er**m b**ir**d c**ur**l.

☞ Write these words under the correct heading below.

| herbs burn third curly stir purple serve burst herd germs dirt dirty turned |
| nurse birth hurt chirp surf service turnip nerve surprise thirsty Thursday |

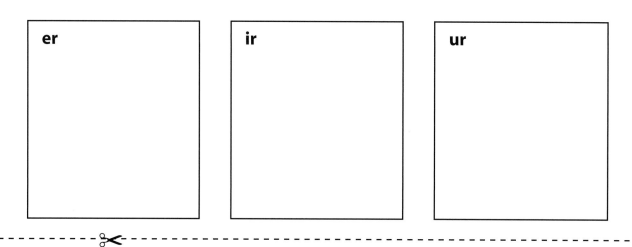

| **er** | **ir** | **ur** |

- - - - - - - - - - - - ✄ -

Challenge!

☞ Cut the top part of the page off and don't look!
   Now complete the words below.

1. "Faster, faster. Keep your n _ _ ve!" shouted the athlete's coach.

2. For the th _ _ d Th _ _ sday in a row he had missed lunch.

3. As he t _ _ ned around, everyone could see the large p _ _ ple bruise on his arm.

4. The n _ _ se walked briskly into the room. "We've banished d _ _ t and g _ _ ms
    from this hospital" she said loudly.

5. The recipe read: Add onion, t _ _ nip and h _ _ bs to the mixture. Pour in stock
    and st _ _ . When ready, s _ _ ve with baked fish.

● Check the words with your lists. How many did you get right?

Check your spelling

Remember these words have the same vowel sound:

f**air**   h**are**   b**ear**.

☞ Write these words under the correct heading below.

wear	fair	parents	fare	flair	upstairs	flare	hare
dairy	spare	tear	aware	hair	repair	pear	scare
pair	bear	beware	bare	careful	swear	share	

air	are	ear

Homophones are words that sound the same but are not spelled the same, for example: fair and fare.

☞ Circle the homophones in your lists. What does each one mean? Tell a partner.

- - - - - - - - - - ✂ -

Challenge!

☞ Cut the top part of the page off and don't look!
Now complete the words below.

w _ _ _   aw _ _ _   sw _ _ _

p _ _ _ nts   c _ _ _ ful   rep _ _ _

sc _ _ _   bew _ _ _   d _ _ _ y

sp _ _ _   sh _ _ _   upst _ _ _ s

● Check the words with your lists. How many did you get right?

Activity sheet – Vowel sounds and 'r'

Sort them out

The are many words with the 'or' sound, but a few are spelled 'oor'.

☞ Write these words under the correct heading.

for	record	sport	floor	acorn	poor
north	sort	flooring	poorly	stormy	moor
door	report	forget	forty	orbit	cork
forbid	sword	morning			

or

oor

Challenge!

☞ Work with a partner. Choose ten words. (Five from each heading.) Learn the words, then test each other.

● Record the words you are not sure of in your spelling bank. Add another word you know with the same sound next to it as a reminder, like this:

Word you are unsure of

forty

Reminder word

*f**or***

English Using phonics

More sorting out

All these words have the 'or' sound, but they are spelled differently.

☞ Write them under the correct heading.

coarse	adore	hoard	shore	score
soar	store	ignore	roar	boar
forecast	hoarse	cupboard	forehead	explore
hoarding	foresee			

ore

oar

Challenge!

☞ Work with a partner. Choose ten words for your partner. (Five from each heading.) They should do the same for you. Learn your spellings, then test each other.

● Record the words you are not sure of in your spelling bank. Add another word you know with the same sound next to it as a reminder, like this:

Word you are unsure of

coarse

Reminder word

*r**oar***

Activity sheet – Vowel sounds and 'r'

Get into gear

When we say the word 'ear' it sounds 'eer'.
Here are other words with the same sounds,
for example: n**ear**, h**ear**, f**ear**, t**ear**, y**ear**.

☞ Add 'ear' to these words and say them. Then match the
words to the clues.

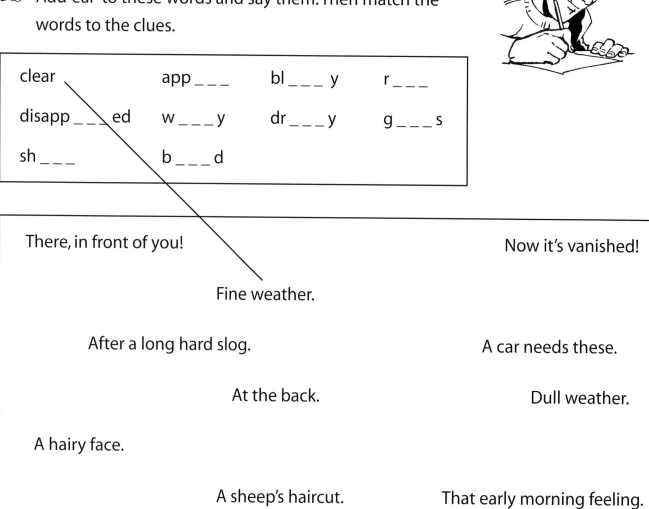

clear   app _ _ _   bl _ _ _ y   r _ _ _

disapp _ _ _ ed   w _ _ _ y   dr _ _ _ y   g _ _ _ s

sh _ _ _   b _ _ _ d

There, in front of you!   Now it's vanished!

Fine weather.

After a long hard slog.   A car needs these.

At the back.   Dull weather.

A hairy face.

A sheep's haircut.   That early morning feeling.

☞ Write sentences with these words to show their meanings.

1. **bleary**

   _____

2. **weary**

   _____

3. **dreary**

   _____

English Using phonics

Teacher's notes

Triple blends/syllables

Objectives

- Learn common word endings
- Learn to identify words with up to three syllables
- Learn to read words beginning with triple blends
- Learn the vowel phonemes 'aw' and 'au'

Prior knowledge

Students should be able to synthesise a range of phoneme blends and endings. They should be able to write sentences and spell some of the words they have learned.

English Framework links

Yr7 Word level 1, 3; Yr8 Word level 1; Yr9 Word level 1

Scottish attainment targets

English Language – Writing
Strand – Knowledge about language
Level D
Strand – Spelling
Level C

Background

Several new features are introduced here: further word endings, triple blends and syllables. Students may already be blending three letters in words of one syllable, such as 'scratch'. They are introduced to longer words here and also to syllable linking of up to three syllables in a word. Students should be able to grasp that words can be split up in this way if you refer to each syllable as a beat. You could reinforce this by introducing a clapping activity, sounding out the syllables with the relevant number of claps. Point out that the word endings covered also provide an extra syllable.

Starter activity

Introduce syllables to students, explaining how words can be broken down and built up. The Activity sheet, 'Danger!', can also be referred to here if you wish.

Activity sheets

In the Activity sheet, 'Making words', students must choose from common word endings to create other words of the same family. Ensure that they understand that not all endings will apply to all words. Note which students create words that are grammatically incorrect but are unaware of this.

Students can work in pairs to complete the Activity sheet, 'Danger!', working out the syllables on their own and checking with each other. The words can also be used as the plot for writing a story at a later date or for homework. It is useful, however, if students discuss potential plots together.

Explain or remind students that we need to blend three letters together at the start of some words. The instructions for the Activity sheet, 'Guessing game', are as follows: *Students will need tokens and a dice. It is best played with two players and an adult. Throw the dice to begin. The player with the highest score starts. One throw only per player. On the word squares the player must say the word correctly using the clues. You should record their scores. The exact throw must be thrown to finish. Players should try to collect as many words as they can.* Several games can be played. The game can also be used as a spelling game. You will need to check that the words students give are correct and supply answers when necessary.

Students should work in pairs to read the Activity sheet 'Shaun Gaunt solves a problem', which deals with the 'au'/'aw' sound. Some words (such as 'undaunted') are challenging. Students should read the whole text before they begin. Ask them to read all the words in bold when the work is completed. You can use the sheet to discuss word meanings and extend students' vocabulary.

The final Activity sheet, 'Lucky stars', includes many words the students should know. There are also a few that may prove trickier. Students can read the sheet in pairs or to you. Note who can read words with the soft 'c' such as 'balance'.

Plenary

Recap on the sounds covered. Check students' ability to split a range of words into syllables and note any additional progress regarding vowel sounds in particular.

Making words

You can make new words by adding endings.

☞ Choose from the endings below to turn these words into new ones.
Write them in the box. The first has been done for you.

talk	loud	snow	rich	sudden	call	weak	poor	think	slow	play	walk

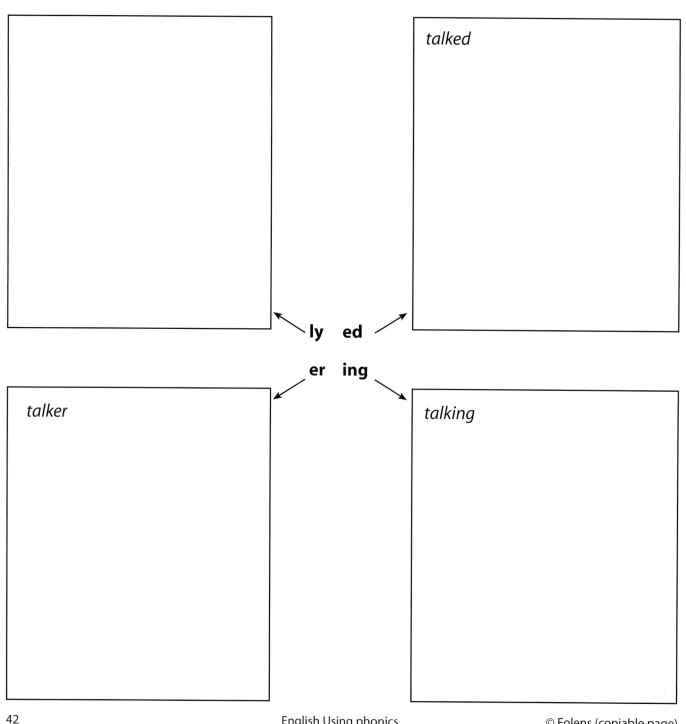

talked

talker

talking

ly   **ed**

er   **ing**

English Using phonics

Activity sheet – Triple blends/syllables

Danger!

A syllable is part of a word.

road	lorry	accident

road	lor	ry	acc	id	ent

1 syllable	2 syllables	3 syllables

☞ Write the number of syllables in the box.

Wednesday	☐	crash	☐
friend	☐	shop	☐
school	☐	window	☐
street	☐	passenger	☐
police	☐	motorist	☐
ambulance	☐	lorry	☐
crossing	☐	witnesses	☐
late	☐	teacher	☐

Guessing game

☞ Play this game with a partner and an adult. You will need three tokens and a dice.

1 ___irrel	2 ___are	3 ___ee	4 MOVE ON 2 SQUARES	5 ___int
6	7 my name is ___uff	8 ___ipe	9 GO BACK 3 SQUARES	10 ___ib
11 banana ___it	12 ___ush	13 ___ong	14 MOVE ON 3 SQUARES	15 ___inter
16 ___ew	17	18 ___edder	19 ___ubbing	20 ___imp
21 GO BACK 4 SQUARES	22 ___ing	23 ___ash	24 ___one	25 ___eam

English Using phonics

Shaun Gaunt solves a problem

☞ Read the following.
The 'au' and aw' words are in bold but ten are missing.
Write them in the correct place.

It was **August. Autumn** would soon be here and

the _ _ _ _ _ _ **Shaun Gaunt** was trying to think of an idea

for a new novel. He **yawned**. He watched a beetle _ _ _ _ _ across his desk. He played with

the remains of a **prawn** sandwich. He **daubed** the sweat from his brow. He felt _ _ _ _ _ .

Ever since his last book **launch** in **Australia** he hadn't been able to think of a thing to

write. He stood up and **sauntered** over to the mirror. He looked at his _ _ _ _ _ _ hair and

brushed a fleck from his **flawless** velvet jacket. Suddenly his _ _ _ dropped.

In the mirror he could see the garden. Sitting on the _ _ _ _ , as plain as day, was a large,

flying _ _ _ _ _ _ . It was bathed in a strange **aura**. Shaun **paused**. He was a **cautious** man.

Should he go out? Then, _ _ _ _ _ _ _ _ _ , he strode towards the craft.

Before he had reached the garden **awning** the top of the spaceship opened up. Out

popped the head of a little man with _ _ _ _ _ green skin. He waved. **Shaun** waved back.

Then everything – the alien, the strange _ _ _ _ , the **saucer** – vanished.

Shaun Gaunt smiled. Now he had the perfect title for his next novel: *An **Awesome** Day*

*in **Dawlish***.

		Word bank		
jaw	crawl	awful	lawn	gaudy
saucer	auburn	undaunted	aura	author

Lucky stars

☞ Read the horoscopes. Underline any words you are not sure of.

Aries The stars are on your side this weekend. Watch out for a surprise on Saturday. A perfect Sunday brings a lucky chance.	**Taurus** A loyal friend will need your advice. Something to do with fried prawns and strawberries?	**Gemini** It's the one you've been waiting for. And what a match it turns out to be!	**Cancer** Ouch! The crab can nip. Don't over-react if a problem comes your way.
Leo You decide to take matters into your own hands. Beware! Your friends think it's a barmy idea.	**Virgo** You're doing just fine. Keep your head and you'll do even better. A chance to impress.	**Libra** Balance. That's your watchword. So stick to that healthy diet (and the odd treat, of course).	**Scorpio** A load of old soap. That's what you think. But search a little further. You'll find pure gold.
Sagittarius Take life by the scruff of the neck and you'll make new friends.	**Capricorn** Don't get moody this weekend. You could miss something you want very badly.	**Aquarius** Water, water everywhere – at least where you're going. Take an umbrella!	**Pisces** Dreaming of faraway places? You win a holiday to Zanzibar.

• Did you know all the words?

Teacher's notes

Silent letters

Objectives

- Learn words that have the silent letters:
  - 'b', 'g' (with 'n') 'k', 'w'; 'l', 'n', 't'
  - 'u' (with 'b' and 'g')
  - 'c' (with 's')
  - 'g' (with 'h') and 'g' (with 'n')

Prior knowledge

Students should know phonemes of one, two and three letters, be able to identify syllables and break down and build up words to deal with a range of silent letters.

English Framework links

Yr7 Word level 1; Yr8 Word level 1; Yr9 Word level 1

Scottish attainment targets

English Language – Writing
Strand – Spelling
Level D

Background

The silent letters covered here range from those that are taught early (for example, silent 'b' in 'comb' and 'bomb') to the more difficult 'u' in words such as 'disguise', 'vogue' and 'antique'. You should therefore select the Activity sheets according to students' progress and performance, whether in reading or spelling.

Starter activity

Explain to students that some letters remain silent when the word is spoken but that they need to be remembered in writing. Find out how much students know by asking them to read the following: 'lamb', 'wrote', 'knot', 'gnat', 'sign', 'walk', 'build', 'scent', 'guard'. (Do not continue if students are struggling early on.) Those that perform well can be given the later sheets to work with.

Activity sheets

In the first two Activity sheets, 'Silent letters (1)' and '(2)', students are encouraged to learn the words as spellings. Silent letters are frequently omitted in writing. However, you can use the Activity sheets to reinforce reading if this suits your purposes better. (The second Activity sheet is more challenging.)

In 'Silent letters (3)' the work is more suitable for teaching or reinforcing reading skills. Students at this level should have reached fluency. Please note that the words 'biscuit' and 'circuit' also have a silent 'u'. These have been omitted to avoid confusion. Depending on students' ability, you may wish to introduce these words. In 'Silent letters (4)', silent 'g' with 'h' and 'n' are covered. The second half of the sheet explores the different sounds of 'ough'. Some 'ough' words will be part of students' everyday vocabulary (such as 'though' and 'through'). However, given the numerous sounds of 'ough', words containing them are notoriously difficult to remember. Students can therefore keep the half-sheet as reference.

The final Activity sheet, 'Words with 'gue' or 'que', deals with these sounds, which also often prove tricky.

Plenary

Note the progress that students have made. For example, give them the short test from the Starter activity (or part of it), but use different words with the same silent letters. Students can record in their word banks any words that have proved difficult during the unit.

Silent letters (1)

These letters are silent in some words: 'b', 'g', 'k', 'w'.

For example: com**b**, **g**nome, **k**not, **w**rap.

☞ Read the words in the box. Underline the silent letters in the words.

Sort the words under the correct silent letter headings.

Put the words in the dustbin that do not have silent letters.

kneel	gnash	blink	lamb	write	knock	written	gnarl
gnat	numb	sword	climb	knack	limb	wander	answer
wren	gnaw	tomb	keeper	bomb	knuckle	golden	

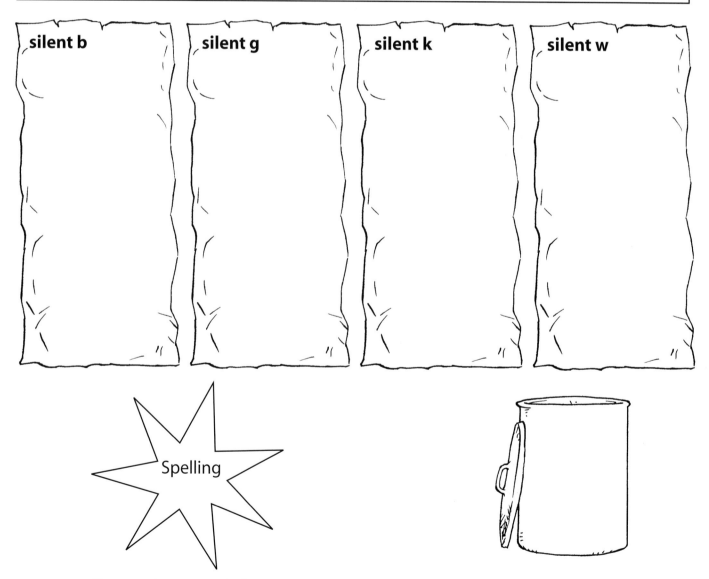

silent b

silent g

silent k

silent w

Spelling

● Choose three words from each list and test your partner.

English Using phonics

Silent letters (2)

These letters are silent in some words: 'l', 'n', 't'.

For example: ha**l**f, hym**n**, cas**t**le.

☞ Read the words in the box. Underline the silent letters in the words.

Sort the words under the correct silent letter headings.

Put the words in the dustbin that do not have silent letters.

stalk	fasten	autumn	nature	listen	folk	column
tablet	rustle	calf	autumnal	tricky	chalk	glisten
solemn	hustle	likeable	calm	condemn		

silent l   silent n   silent t

Spelling

• Choose four words from each list and test your partner.

Silent letters (3)

The letter 'c' is silent in some words. For example, with 's' in 's**c**ience'.

The letter 'u' is silent in some words. For example, in 'b**u**ild' and 'g**u**ard'.

☞ Read the words in the box. Underline the silent letters in the words.

Sort the words under the correct silent letter headings.

Put the words in the dustbin that do not have silent letters.

guess	scene	build	gutter	scientist	guided
built	scissors	builder	scraped	guitar	sceptre
guy	cutting	scenery	buckle	scent	guarantee

silent c

silent u

● Underline any words you do not understand. Find out their meanings.

English Using phonics

Silent letters (4)

The 'g' is silent in all these words. Sometimes it is with 'gh' and sometimes with 'gn'.

Read each word.

1.   Underline the silent letters, 'gh' and 'gn'.

2.   Draw up two lists headed 'gh' and 'gn' and write the words in the correct lists.

sign	light	tonight	reign	sighed	delight	high	consign	midnight
resign	tight	right	lightning	design	mighty	twilight	slight	align

3.   Finish this limerick

There once was a handsome young kni _ _ t,

With helmet and sword polished bri _ _ t,

But the thought of a fi _ _ t,

Made him quiver with fri _ _ t,

So alas! He was always in fli _ _ t.

✂ ---

The 'gh' is also silent in words that have 'ough'.

But 'ough' has seven different sounds!

Read all these words. Keep this in your word bank.

Add words as you need to.

pl**ough** (like 'ow' in 'cow')

th**rough** (like 'ew' in 'threw')

en**ough** (like 'uff' in 'cuff')   '**ough**'   bo**ught** (like 'aw' in jaw)

th**ough** (like 'oe' in 'toe')   r**ough** (like 'u' in 'but')   c**ough** (like 'off')

Words with 'gue' or 'que'

The 'ue' is silent in words ending 'gue', like 'prologue'. We sound 'gue' as 'g'.

The 'ue' is also slient in words ending 'que', like 'antique'. We sound 'que' as 'k'.

☞ Read the words in the box. Underline 'gue' and 'que'.

Sort the words into the correct list.

rogue	unique	fatigue	cheque	picturesque	plague	league
colleague	mosque	oblique	catalogue	technique	prologue	
grotesque	epilogue	intrigue	tongue			

prologue	**antique**

● Record the words you do not understand. Find out their meanings with a partner.

English Using phonics

Teacher's notes

Soft and hard sounds

Objectives

- Learn soft 'c' and 'g'
- Learn 'ph' sounding 'f'
- Learn:
  – 'ch' sounding 'k',
  – 'ch' sounding 'sh'
- Recall the common 'ch' sound

Prior knowledge

Students should be able to synthesise a range of phonemes, blends and endings. They should know what syllables are and be able to break down words as well as build them up. They should be able to write sentences and spell some of the words they have learned.

English Framework links

Yr7 Word level 1; Yr8 Word level 1; Yr9 Word level 1

Scottish attainment targets

English Language – Writing
Strand – Spelling
Level D

Background

Soft 'c' can occur at the beginning, middle and end of words but is most often found at the end, following a long vowel to make words such as 'face' or 'advance'. Soft 'g' is more common at the middle and end of words and often occurs when followed by 'y', 'e' and 'i' at the beginning of words (though by no means always, for example, 'get', 'give'). The other soft sound, 'ph', sounding 'f', is Greek in origin and also occurs at the beginning, middle and end of words.

It is assumed that students working with the 'ch' sound will be aware of it in words such as 'chop' and 'chip'. It is recalled here in longer words for students to make the comparison with the other 'ch' sounds.

Starter activity

Introduce students to soft 'c' and ask them to think of some common words that have the sound at the end of the word. Give them an example: 'ace'. Other words might be: 'ice', 'race', 'mice', 'dice', 'space', 'place' and 'dance'. If students have a good knowledge of these words introduce soft 'g', explaining that it sounds like 'j'. Point out that in English, words do not end with 'j'. You can refer to words such as: 'age', 'page', 'rage' and also 'gin' and 'gem'.

Activity sheets

The Activity sheets, 'The office', 'Grimini the Magician' and 'Dolphins' all follow the same pattern. They can be used individually or consecutively according to a student's progress. Remind students that the sound may occur more than once in a word. Once students have selected the appropriate words for their lists, ask them to read them to you and to underline where the soft sound occurs in the word. For example, in 'circle' it would be at the beginning, in 'practice' at the beginning and the end and in 'office' at the end. This can help students to recall spellings.

The multiple 'ch' sound is separated into two Activity sheets, 'That old chestnut' and 'A toothache and a headache', since many of the words are tricky. Picture clues are given for some words. (Please note, you could explain the saying, 'That old chestnut', referring to the 'ch' blend and how it occurs in different words as different sounds, for example 'ch' as in 'chip', 'ch' as in 'chemist'.)

Plenary

Check students' lists of names and share them with the group. Recap on the sounds covered. Students can also carry out peer assessments.

The office

1. Read the words in the computer screen.

2. Make a list in the empty screen of all the soft 'c' words.

3. Underline in red any words you don't know.

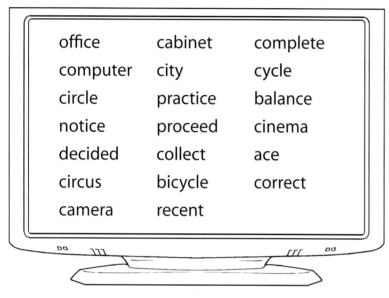

office	cabinet	complete
computer	city	cycle
circle	practice	balance
notice	proceed	cinema
decided	collect	ace
circus	bicycle	correct
camera	recent	

4. Think of names that have a soft 'c' in them. Do any people in your class have names with a soft 'c'?

5. On another sheet of paper, write a short email to someone in an office about work. Use these words: *recent notice decided.*

Grimini the Magician

1. Read the words in the wizard's book.
2. Make a list in the chest of all the soft 'g' words.
3. Underline in red any words you don't know.

huge	manage	rage	magic
damage	together	gym	giant
glimmer	grinning	postage	ginger
growing	age	grave	message
garage	going	golden	

4. Does the name the Grimini the Magician have soft or hard 'g's?
5. Think of names that have a soft 'g' in them. Do any people in your class have names with a soft 'g'?
6. Choose three soft 'g' words from your list. Write one sentence with them all in.

Activity sheet – Soft and hard sounds

Dolphins

1.   Read the words in the dolphin.

2.   Make a list in the empty sea of all the 'ph' words.

3.   Underline in red any words you don't know.

4.   Work with a partner. Take it in turns to explain what each 'ph' word means.

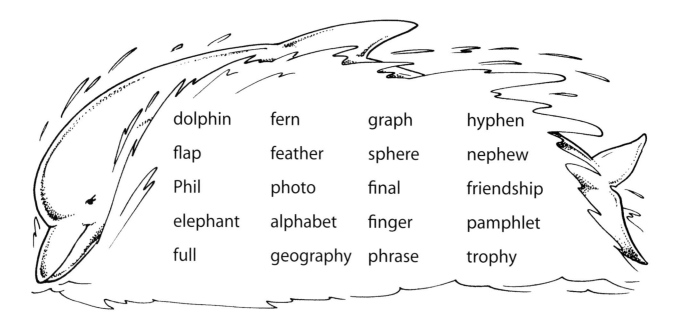

dolphin	fern	graph	hyphen
flap	feather	sphere	nephew
Phil	photo	final	friendship
elephant	alphabet	finger	pamphlet
full	geography	phrase	trophy

5.   Think of names that have a soft 'ph' in them. Do any people in your class have names with a soft 'ph'?

English Using phonics   © Folens (copiable page)

Activity sheet – Soft and hard sounds

That old chestnut

1. Match the words to the pictures.

chipmunk	brochure	chauffeur	parachute	chestnut	chute

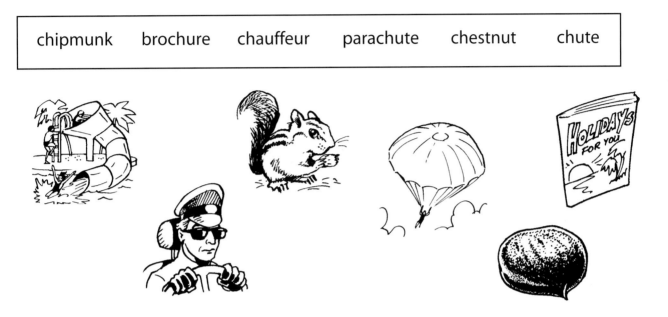

2. Read these words.

machine	chess	lunch	charm	Richard	chicken	orchard	chef	Michelle	church

3. Write the words in the correct lists below.

ch (like chip)

ch (sounding sh)

A toothache and a headache

1. Match the words to the pictures.

| choir | stomach | architect | arch | mechanic | chemistry | orchestra | chocolate |

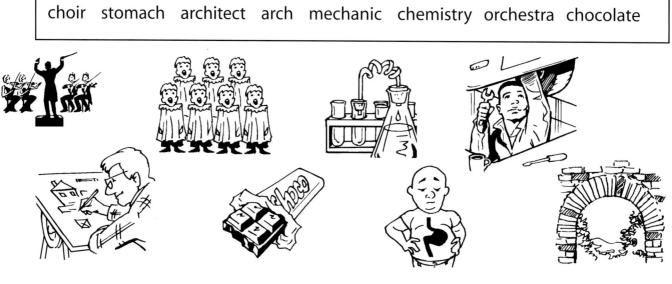

2. Read these words.

| school | Christmas | toothache | bench | headache | cherry |
| orchid | chemist | chocolate | scheme | channel |

3. Write the words in the correct lists below.

ch (like chip)

ch (sounding k)

Teacher's notes

Prefixes and suffixes

Objectives

- Learn that prefixes are words placed in front of words to extend them and create new words
- Learn that suffixes are words placed at the end of words to extend them and create new words
- Learn that prefixes and suffixes are syllables
- Learn the meanings of prefixes and suffixes

Prior knowledge

Students should have achieved good phonic knowledge and reading experience, be able to identify syllables and break down and build up words. They should be able to spell words of two syllables or more.

English Framework links

Yr7 Word level 1, 3, 4; Yr8 Word level 1; Yr9 Word level 1

Scottish attainment targets

English Language – Reading
Strand – Knowledge about language
Level E
Strand – Spelling
Level C

Background

Students are likely to know several prefixes and suffixes in simple words. For example, 'un' is a common prefix usually learned early and is added to words such as 'tie' to make 'untie'. They will also have gathered that 'un' changes the meaning of a word to its opposite. However, they are less likely to know or may confuse other prefixes, for example by mistakenly using 'un' to create opposites when the prefix should be 'ir', 'il', 'mis' and others.

Starter activity

Discuss how prefixes function and point out that:
- some prefixes can be attached to existing words (see example in Background above), while others cannot
- prefixes change the meaning of the root word
- prefixes do not change the spelling of the root word.

Activity sheets

The first Activity sheet, 'Prefix meanings', introduces prefixes to students and focuses on meaning. It also includes antonyms. Students can work in pairs or you could use the sheet for group work, discussing the possible meanings of the words. Students should be able to work out 'biped' since both prefixes 'bi' and 'ped' are included. You could ask them to give an example of a two-footed creature and note whether they deduce that humans are bipeds.

The two following Activity sheets, 'Prefixes' and 'Suffixes', provide common prefixes and suffixes for students to think of or find their own words.

The final Activity sheet, 'Syllable linking', focuses on words of three syllables. Students are also asked to create new words using prefixes and suffixes.

Plenary

Discuss students' new words from 'Syllable linking' in a group. Rather than provide the meanings, students should just read their words and ask others to guess their meanings. Recap on the work covered in the lesson.

Activity sheet – Prefixes and suffixes

Prefix meanings

☞ Below are the meanings of some prefixes.

Use them to work out what the words might mean.

Check the words in a dictionary.

Prefix	Meaning	Word	Word meaning
aqua	*water*	aquatic	_____
bi	*two*	biped	_____
centi	*hundred*	centurion	_____
hyper	*too much*	hyperactive	_____
mal	*bad*	malfunction	_____
micro	*small*	microbe	_____
octo	*eight*	octette	_____
ped	*foot*	pedicure	_____
photo	*light*	photon	_____
sub	*under*	submariner	_____

● Some prefixes can change words into their opposite meanings or **antonyms**.

☞ Add the right prefix to the words below to make antonyms. Check the words in a dictionary. Were you right?

Prefixes	il	in	ir	dis	mis	un

Words	Antonyms
healthy	_____
regular	_____
agree	_____
visible	_____
understand	_____
logical	_____

English Using phonics

Activity sheet – Prefixes and suffixes

Prefixes

☞ Make words from these prefixes.

   Write them out.

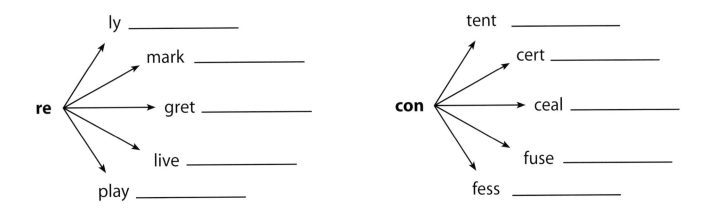

☞ Make words from these prefixes, choosing your own words.

   Use a dictionary to help you.

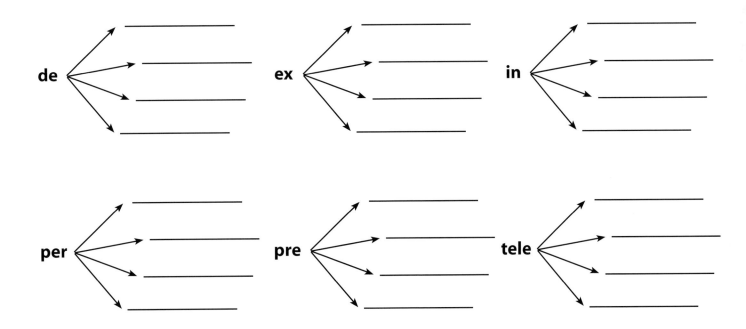

• Do you know the meaning of all the words? Check them.

English Using phonics

Suffixes

☞ Read what these suffixes mean.

Suffix	Meaning
- ant or - ent	what someone is or does
- graph	written
- proof	not affected by
- scope	for looking closely at something
- ship	skill
- phobia	fear of something

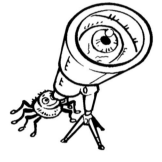

☞ Which suffixes go with these pairs of words? Write them down.
Find the words you don't know in a dictionary.

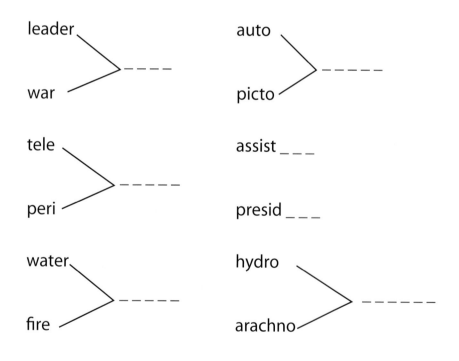

leader
war
} _ _ _ _

auto
picto
} _ _ _ _ _

tele
peri
} _ _ _ _ _

assist _ _ _

presid _ _ _

water
fire
} _ _ _ _ _

hydro
arachno
} _ _ _ _ _

English Using phonics

Activity sheet – Prefixes and suffixes

Syllable linking

☞ Begin with the syllables on the left.

Match them to the correct syllables in the second and third columns to make words.

Write the word in the last column. The first has been done for you.

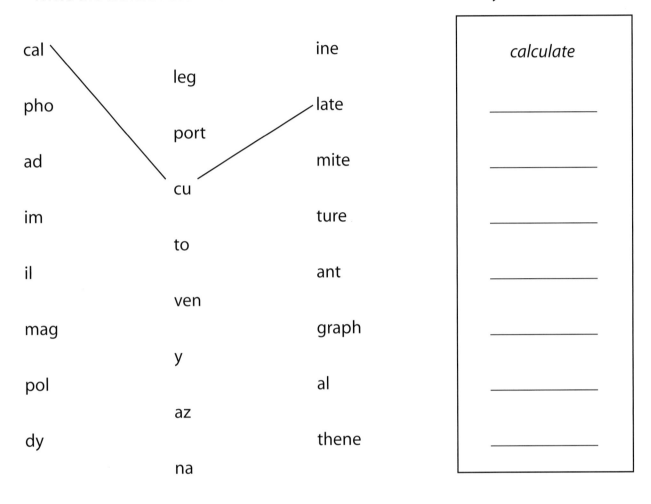

cal	ine		*calculate*
	leg		
pho		late	_____
	port		
ad		mite	_____
	cu		
im		ture	_____
	to		
il		ant	_____
	ven		
mag		graph	_____
	y		
pol		al	_____
	az		
dy		thene	_____
	na		

● Underline any words you don't know. Check their meanings.

☞ Make up new words using prefixes and suffixes!
Study the Activity sheet, 'Prefix meanings'.
For example:

● *malped* meaning *bad foot.*

Assessment sheet

Tick the boxes to show what you know or can do.

	know/ yes	not sure/ sometimes	don't know/ no
1. I listen to the teacher.			
2. I can work well with a partner.			
3. I can work well in a group.			
4.			
5.			
6.			
7.			
8.			
9.			
10.			

I know best/I can do best:

....

....

I need to: **(Write no more than three targets.)**

....

....

....